Creative Art & Activities

Crayons, Chalk, and Markers

Mary Mayesky

THOMSON

DELMAR LEARNING

Australia   Canada   Mexico   Singapore   Spain   United Kingdom   United States

THOMSON

DELMAR LEARNING

Creative Art and Activities: Crayons, Chalk, and Markers
Mary Mayesky

Vice President, Career Ed SBU:
Dawn Gerrain

Director of Editorial:
Sherry Gomoll

Acquisitions Editor:
Erin O'Connor

Developmental Editor:
Alexis Ferraro

Editorial Assistant:
Ivy Ip

Director of Production:
Wendy A. Troeger

Production Coordinator:
Nina Tucciarelli

Composition:
Stratford Publishing Services

Director of Marketing:
Donna J. Lewis

Cover Design:
Tom Cicero

Library of Congress Cataloging-in-Publication
Data

Mayesky, Mary

1-4018-3473-6

NOTICE TO THE READER

Publisher does not warrant or guarantee any of the products described herein or perform any independent analysis in connection with any of the product information contained herein. Publisher does not assume, and expressly disclaims, any obligation to obtain and include information other than that provided to it
by the manufacturer.

The reader is expressly warned to consider and adopt all safety precautions that might be indicated by the activities herein and to avoid all potential hazards. By
following the instructions contained herein, the reader willingly assumes all risks in connection with such instructions.

The Publisher makes no representation or warranties of any kind, including but not limited to, the warranties of fitness for particular purpose or merchantabil-
ity, nor are any such representations implied with respect to the material set forth herein, and the publisher takes no responsibility with respect to such material. The publisher shall not be liable for any special, consequential, or exemplary damages resulting, in whole or part, from the readers' use of, or reliance upon,
this material.

To Claire,

my first creation, my constant inspiration.

With love, Mom

Contents

Introduction

Welcome to the world of crayons, chalk, and markers! As the activities in this book show, these are more than just traditional art materials. Crayons, chalk, and markers are art materials full of creative possibilities!

Crayons are the most basic, most familiar, and easiest tool for young children to use. Large crayons are easy to hold and can make attractive marks on paper. Crayon drawing is an excellent opportunity for creative picture marking. Using crayons, children can tell stories visually, as they feel them. Most young children have crayons, but they often only use them to draw on paper. As this book shows, crayons can engage children's interest in many other ways. The creative uses of crayons in this book inspire many other unique uses for them.

Like crayons, chalk has endless creative possibilities. It is inexpensive and comes in various colors. Most people think of using chalk only on a chalkboard, but, as this book shows, chalkboard is but one of the many surfaces on which to use chalk. As you use the activities in this book, you will surely develop new and different surfaces for chalk creations.

Felt-tip markers are excellent tools for creative activities. They provide clear, quick, easily made, and nice-looking marks. Because felt-tip markers require little pressure to make bold marks, they are excellent tools for the youngest artists. Though this book emphasizes crayons and chalk, many activities include markers, as well.

The activities in this book are designed for children aged 2 through 8. An icon representing a suggested age for the activity is listed at the top of each activity. However, use your knowledge of the child's abilities to guide you in choosing and using the activities in this book. Wherever appropriate, information is provided on how to adapt the activity for children over age 8.

The focus of this book is a creative approach to using crayons, chalk, and markers. The activities are meant to be starting points for exploring this art form. Both you and the children are encouraged to explore, experiment, and enjoy the world of crayons, chalk, and markers.

GETTING STARTED

Process vs. Product

The focus of this book and all early childhood art activities is the process, not the product. This means that the process of creating, not the product, is the main reason for the activity. The joys of creating, exploring materials, and discovering how things look and work are all part of the creative process. How the product looks, what it is "supposed to be," is unimportant to the child, and it should be unimportant to the adult.

Young children delight in the experience, the exploration, and the experimentation of art activities. The adult's role is to provide interesting materials and an environment that encourages children's creativity. Stand back when you are tempted to "help" children in their art activities. Instead, encourage all children to discover their own unique abilities.

Starting with Crayons, Chalk, and Markers

In their first attempts at using crayons, young children usually work randomly. This first step is normally called "scribbling." At the very beginning, early scribblers scribble for the sheer joy of the movement. There is little concern for making scribbles in any particular direction or shape.

As children become more and more involved with crayoning, they gradually develop the physical skills to control their scribbles. As this stage, they scribble purposefully in one direction or another.

As children develop motor control and hand-eye coordination, and when they have a chance to use crayons regularly, they are gradually able to make simple forms: lines, circles, ovals, squares, and rectangles. As their motor control and hand-eye coordination continue to develop, children can combine these simple forms into figures, such as stick figures, trees, and houses. Combining these simple figures, a child can make a picture. This is an important step, because children can express their feelings and ideas visually on the paper. It is a long way from those first random scribbles!

The process is much the same with chalk and markers—from random scribbling through controlled scribbles to basic forms and finally to picture making. Of the two, young artists use chalk less commonly, perhaps because chalk is brittle and easily broken. It is also impermanent, smearing very easily. However, there are some effective ways to incorporate chalk into young children's artwork. These ideas are covered in later sections.

Considering the Child

Young children find it hard to wait patiently to use materials in an activity. Often, the excitement of creativity and patience do not mix. In addition, it is sometimes difficult for young children to share. With young children, plan to have enough crayons, markers, and chalk for each child's use. For example, have a good supply of markers so that each child can use colors without waiting. Ample supplies encourage creative activities.

Gathering Materials

Each activity in this book includes a list of required materials. It is important to gather all materials before starting an activity with children. Children's creative experiences are easily discouraged when they must sit and wait while the adult looks for the tape, extra scissors, or colored paper. Be sure to gather materials in a place children can easily access.

Storing and Making Materials Available

Having the appropriate crayons and markers for artwork is not enough. These materials must be stored and readily accessible to the children. For example, jumbling crayons, markers, and chalk together in a basket is not ideal. Instead, place the materials in separate boxes so that each child has an individual, complete set. This system reduces arguments and ensures that all colors are available to all children as needed.

Another option is to store the materials in a clear-plastic box that is shallow enough for children to easily search. Some teachers find clear-plastic shoeboxes invaluable for storing children's chalk, crayons, and markers. Such containers, which are available at economy stores, are great for storing and stacking all kinds of art materials. Yet another alternative is to store crayons or markers in wide-mouth containers according to color: all red crayons in one container, all blue in another, and so on.

Be creative when thinking about how to store and make available materials for your little artists. Storing supplies in handy boxes and other containers makes creating art, and cleaning up afterward, more fun! **Figure 1** gives some added hints for storing materials.

Using Food Products

Several activities involve the use of different kinds of foods. There are long-standing arguments for and against food use in art activities. For example, many teachers have long used potato printing as a traditional printing activity for young children. These teachers feel that potatoes are an economical way to prepare printing objects for children. Using potatoes beyond their shelf life is an alternative to throwing them away. On the other hand, many teachers feel that food is for eating and should be used for nothing else.

This book has many activities that do not use food so that there will be options for teachers who oppose food use in art activities. Also, where possible, alternatives to food items are suggested. Whatever your opinion, creative activities in printing are provided for your and the children's exploration and enjoyment.

Employing Safe Materials

For all the activities in this book and in any art activities for young children, be sure to use safe art supplies. Read labels on all art materials. Check materials for age appropriateness. The Art and Creative Materials Institute (ACMI) labels art materials AP (approved product) and CL (certified label). Products with these labels are certified safe for use by young children. The ACMI provides an extensive list of materials and manufacturers of safe materials for all young children. This information is available on the ACMI Web site at http://www.acminet.org or by writing to 715 Boylston Street, Boston, MA 02116.

Some basic safety hints for art activities are:

- Always use products that are appropriate for the child. Use nontoxic materials for children in Grades 6 and lower.
- Never use products for skin painting or food preparation unless the products are intended for those uses.
- Keep art materials in their original containers. Do not transfer art materials to other containers. You will lose the valuable safety information on the product packages.
- Do not eat or drink while using art and craft materials. Wash after use. Clean yourself and your supplies.
- Be sure that your work area is well ventilated.

FIGURE 1 · TIPS FOR STORING ART MATERIALS

The ways materials, supplies, and space are arranged can make or break children's and teachers' art experiences. Following are suggestions for arranging supplies for art experiences:

1. *Scissor holders.* Holders can be made from gallon milk or bleach containers. Simply punch holes in the containers and place scissors in the holes with the scissor points to the inside. Egg cartons turned upside down with slits in each mound also make excellent holders.

2. *Paint containers.* Containers can range from muffin tins and plastic egg cartons to plastic soft-drink cartons with baby food jars in them. These work especially well outdoors as well as indoors, because they are large and not easily tipped. Place one brush in each container. This prevents colors from mixing and makes cleanup easier.

3. *Crayon containers.* Juice and vegetable cans painted or covered with contact paper work very well.

4. Crayon pieces may be melted in muffin trays in a warm oven. These pieces, when cooled, are nice for rubbings or drawings. Crayola® makes a unit that is designed specifically for melting crayons safely.

5. Printing with tempera is easier if the tray is lined with a sponge or a paper towel.

6. A card file for art activities helps organize the program.

7. *Clay containers.* Airtight coffee cans and plastic food containers are excellent ways to keep clay moist and always ready for use.

8. *Paper scrap boxes.* By keeping two or more boxes of scrap paper of different sizes, children will be able to choose the size paper they want more easily.

9. Cover a wall area with pegboard and suspend heavy shopping bags or transparent plastic bags from hooks inserted in the pegboard to hold miscellaneous art supplies. Hang smocks in the same way on the pegboard (at child level, of course).

10. Use the back of a piano or bookcase to hang a shoe bag. Its pockets can hold many small items.

11. Use divided frozen food trays or a revolving lazy Susan to hold miscellaneous small items.

(From Mayesky, Mary. *Creative Activites for Young Children*, 7th ed., Clifton Park, NY: Delmar Learning.)

Potentially unsafe paper-art supplies include the following:

- *Epoxy, instant glues, or other solvent-based glues.* Use only water-based white glue.
- *Paints that require solvents like turpentine to clean.* Use only water-based paints.
- *Cold water or commercial dyes that contain chemical additives.* Use only natural vegetable dyes made from beets, onion skins, and so on.

- *Permanent markers*. Permanent markers may contain toxic solvents. Use only water-based markers.

Be aware of all children's allergies. Children with allergies to wheat, for example, may be irritated by the wheat paste used in papier-mâché. Children allergic to peanuts must taste nothing with peanut butter. In fact, some centers make it a rule to avoid peanut butter use in food or art activities. Other art materials that may cause allergic reactions include chalk or other dusty substances, water-based clay, and any material that contains petroleum products.

Also be aware of children's habits. Some young children put everything in their mouths. (This can be the case at any age.) Others may be shy and slow to accept new materials. Use your knowledge of children's tendencies to help you plan art activities that are safe for all children.

Take the time to talk with the children about which things they may taste and which they may not. For example, when making anything mixed with glue, remind the children that glue is not to be tasted. You may find it helpful to use a large cutout of a smiley face with a tongue at the end of the smile to indicate an "edible activity." Make a copy of the smiley face and place a large black X over it to show a "no-taste activity."

Using Crayons—Basics

Crayons are an ideal medium for children: They are bold, colorful, clean, and inexpensive. They consist of an oily or a waxy binder mixed with color pigments. They are of various types; some are soft, some are semihard, and some (kindergarten or "fat" crayons) are for general use with young children. Crayons work well on most papers, but they do not blend well. Attempts to blend crayon often tear the paper.

Many different types of crayons are available. There are special crayons for use on construction paper, there are washable crayons, and there are fabric crayons, to name just a few. All these crayons are great to try with children, but if you have a limited budget, traditional wax crayons work well for most activities. However, be sure to buy good-quality, wax crayons. Good-quality crayons like Crayola® crayons hold up to children's frequent and hard use. Inexpensive crayons create less successful crayon experiences for children.

Children may use crayons on a wide assortment of surfaces, including newsprint, wrapping paper, newspaper, construction paper, corrugated cardboard, cloth, and wood. Crayons work well on most papers. Crayons can be applied thinly to produce semitransparent layers of subtle color, and they can be coated with black paint and scratched through for crayon etching.

Understanding Crayons at Different Stages

Toddlers and children just beginning to scribble need crayons that are safe and easy to hold and use. Large, nontoxic crayons are good tools for young scribblers. A good-grade, kindergarten-type crayon is the best tool for this stage. The crayon should be large and unwrapped so it can be used on both the sides and the ends. Good-quality crayons are strong enough to hold up to rough first scribbles. They also make bright, clear colors, which appeal to children.

Young artists use their whole arms, as well as their hands and fingers, when using crayons or markers. For this reason, early scribblers should use large, white paper.

Crayon scribbles show better on white paper, so children can see more easily the results of their scribbling. The want-ad section of the newspaper is also appropriate paper for beginning artists. The advertisements' small print makes a neutral, nonintrusive background for scribbling. In addition, this section of the paper provides a generous supply of material for young scribblers. This, in turn, encourages children to scribble more often.

Young scribblers need only a few crayons at a time. Too many crayons may distract children during scribbling. At this point, the process of scribbling, not the color of the crayon, is the main point of the activity. A box of 32 crayons, for example, could become an object of exploration and thus a distraction from scribbling. A new color may be added when a new drawing is started.

As preschool children develop more motor skills and can scribble purposefully, they hold their tools more like adults and have growing control of their materials. Preschool children at this point can now control their scribbles, making loops, circles, and lines that are distinguishable and can be repeated at will.

Preschool children in this stage have enough motor control and hand-eye coordination to use smaller crayons. A variety of papers can be used, from newsprint to construction paper. It is not as necessary to have the largest paper, because the child can now control the crayon on a smaller surface. Papers of many sizes, shapes, and colors are appropriate for children at this stage.

When children can make pictures with crayons, the larger the variety of paper and crayons, the better! A box of 32 crayons is perfect for a young artist at this stage. Challenge the children with new and different colors of paper and crayons. Make some crayons of your own using the Crayon Cupcakes activity. There are limitless creative possibilities with crayons.

School-age children also benefit from using crayons. The fact that crayons were introduced to these children at a younger age may lead the children to think that crayons are beneath the dignity of older artists, but this is not the case. Examples abound of distinguished drawings made in this medium, as far back as the nineteenth century. Miro and Picasso used crayons in their work, so, do not neglect this material with your more "grown-up" artists!

Using Crayons—Processes

Encourage the children to experiment with crayons and to use different parts of the crayon. Through these experiments, the children will discover new methods that satisfy their needs for expression. The wax crayon has great versatility and can be used in many different ways:

- Make thin lines with the point of the crayon, heavy lines with the blunt end or the side.

- Vary the pressure to create subtle tints or solid, brilliant colors.

- Make rough texture by using broken lines, dots, jabs, dashes, and other strokes with the point.

- Create smooth texture by using the flat side or by drawing lines close together in the same direction with the point.

- Twist, turn, and swing the crayon in arcs, and move it in various ways to achieve different effects.
- Repeat motions to create a rhythm or pattern.

Avoid small pieces of paper and patterned artwork or coloring books. Asking children to color patterned artwork undermines the children's creativity. Children who are frequently given patterns to cut out or outlines to color are in fact being told that their own artwork is inadequate. For example, a pattern of a dog for children to color in or cut out says to them—more clearly than words could—that, "This is what your drawing should look like; this is the *right* way to make a dog. You and the way you might draw a dog aren't good enough."

Using Chalk—Basics

Children are often given chalk with a blackboard, but young children seem to use it ineffectively there. Young children do better when they can mark on the sidewalk with chalk, perhaps because the rougher texture of the cement more easily pulls the color off the chalk stick. The children seem more able to tell what they are doing as they squat and draw. It is, of course, necessary to explain to the children that they may draw with chalk only on special places.

Some young artists apply chalk in separate strokes, letting the color blend in the viewer's eye. Others are not reluctant to blend the colors and do so successfully, although the colors may get muddied. Of course, there is no need to caution children against this. They should be encouraged to explore by rubbing with the fingers, cotton swabs, or anything available. Most children will select and use chalk easily, However, chalk is too brittle for toddlers' early scribbling.

Chalk is inexpensive and available in several forms. Typical blackboard chalk is appropriate for using on blackboards and in art projects. Some chalk, made specifically for chalk drawings, is more expensive but worth the cost because it produces rich and vibrant colors. Another form of chalk is sidewalk chalk.

This chalk is commonly available during summer months at most commodity stores. Sidewalk chalk, which is designed to wash away with water, usually has a detergent component. It is also larger than regular chalk, which makes it easier to use on cement. Sidewalk chalk is inexpensive and is available in a good range of colors. Crayola makes a liquid sidewalk chalk that can be brushed directly onto cement.

Using Chalk—Processes

The following basic information can help you successfully incorporate chalk into art activities for young children:

- Chalk drawing is best done on a paper with a slightly coarse, abrasive surface. This texture helps the paper trap and hold the chalk particles. Many papers have this quality, including inexpensive manila paper.
- Chalks are brittle and break easily. They are also impermanent, smearing very easily. The teacher, with proper ventilation, should spray completed works with a "fixative" (ordinary hairspray works well).
- Chalk strokes can be strengthened by wetting the chalk or paper.

- Various liquids can be used with chalks for interesting results. These include dipping the chalk sticks in buttermilk, starch, and sugar water.
- Liquid tends to seal the chalk, so you must occasionally rub a piece of old sandpaper on the end of the chalk to break this seal and allow the color to come off again.

Using Markers—Basics

Markers are popular tools for young artists. They are especially good for children who have progressed through the scribble stage and can make basic shapes. Markers require little pressure to make bold marks and basic shapes. They should be nontoxic and water soluble so that most spots can be washed out of the children's clothes. One drawback of markers is lost tops. A marker will dry out fairly quickly without its top. See **Figure 2**, Marker Maintenance, for some suggestions on how to prolong the life of colored markers.

As with crayon use, children's progression from random scribbling through controlled scribbling to basic forms and then picture making applies to marker use. However, markers are not suggested for beginning scribblers, because they can only be used one way. Unlike crayons, which can be used on the sides, top, and bottom, markers are a one-way (top-only) tool.

Once children can control their scribbles, markers are an appropriate tool. Markers produce attractive lines and shapes. Children enjoy seeing their marks come out as desired and in such a colorful way. Markers make great tools for picture making, as well. Be sure to have colored markers in many colors and tip widths for picture making. Also, be sure the markers are not permanent.

Using Markers—Processes

Colored markers come in beautiful, clear colors. Some markers even have scents! Glittery markers are another treat for young artists. Compared with paint, markers have the additional advantage of staying bright and clear until the children exhaust them.

Some basic materials to use with markers are:

- *Sturdy sheets of paper (manila or newsprint, 8" × 12" or 12" × 18").* Spread the paper on a table or on the floor, or pin it to a wall or an easel. Paper of different shapes and colors may be used for variety.
- A *basket of colored markers in many colors and tip widths.* See the preceding "Storing Tips for Art Materials" section for ways to organize markers effectively.
- *Colored pens and pencils for older children to incorporate with their marker drawings.*

Creating a Child-Friendly Environment

It is difficult to be creative when you have to worry about keeping yourself and your work area clean. Cover all artwork areas with newspaper. It is best to tape the paper to the surface to avoid having markers or other materials seep through the spaces. In addition, picking up a messy newspaper and throwing it away is so much easier than cleaning up a tabletop! Other coverups that work well are shower curtains and plastic tablecloths.

Remember to cover the children, too! Some good child coverups are men's shirts (with the sleeves cut off), aprons, pillowcases with holes cut for the head and arms, and

FIGURE 2 · MARKER MAINTENANCE

Markers are wonderful for young artists. But busy artists frequently lose caps from these markers, often resulting in dried-out markers. Replacing dried-out markers can be expensive, so here are a few hints on "marker maintenance" to help preserve them as long as possible.

- Solve the lost cap/dry-out problem by setting the caps with *open ends up* in a margarine or whipped topping container filled with plaster of Paris. Make sure the plaster does not cover the holes in the caps. When the plaster dries, the markers can be put into the caps and will stand upright until ready for use again.

- Give new life to old, dry felt markers by storing them *tips down with the caps on*. When the markers become dried out, remove the caps and put in a few drops of water. This usually helps "revive" them.

- Recycle dried-out markers by having children dip them in paint and use them for drawing.

- Make your own pastel markers by adding dry tempera paint (or food color) to bottles of white shoe polish that come with sponge applicator tops.

- Use empty plastic shoe polish bottles or roll-on deodorant bottles to make your own markers. Wash the tops and bottles thoroughly and fill them with watery tempera paint.

(From Mayesky, Mary. *Creative Activites for Young Children*, 7th ed., Clifton Park, NY: Delmar Learning.)

smocks. Some fun alternatives to these are sets of old clothes or shoes that can be worn as "art clothes." These old clothes could become "art journals" as they became covered with the traces of various art projects.

Creating a Child's Art Environment

Encourage young artists by displaying appropriate art prints and other works of art. Do not make the mistake of thinking young children do not enjoy "grown-up" art. Children are never too young to enjoy the colors, lines, patterns, and designs of artists' work. Art posters from a local museum, for example, can brighten an art area. Such posters also get children looking and talking about art, which encourages their creativity.

Display pieces of pottery, shells and rocks, and other beautiful objects from nature to encourage children's appreciation of the lines, symmetries, and colors of nature. These design concepts are part of the drawing experience. Even the youngest child can enjoy the look and feel of smooth, colored rocks and the beauty of fall leaves. All these are natural parts of a child's world that can be talked about with young children as those children create artwork. Beautiful objects encourage creativity.

Now, enter the world of crayons, chalk, and markers in the pages that follow. Enjoy the trip!

A

All Ages

Basic Crayon Rubbings

MATERIALS

☐ newsprint or other light-type paper

☐ unwrapped crayons

☐ objects to rub over (e.g., paper clips, leaves, coins, rickrack)

HELPFUL HINTS

- Rubbings are a good activity, even for very young artists, because they require a lesser degree of small motor development in the fingers and hands.

- For 2-year-olds, the objects rubbed over need to be large and too big to put in the mouth.

DEVELOPMENTAL GOALS

Develop creativity, small motor development, and hand-eye coordination and explore a new crayoning technique.

PREPARATION

Talk about the collection of objects for this activity. Discuss shape and size.

PROCESS

1. Place the paper over an object.

2. Color hard over the object with the side of the crayon.

3. Repeat the process with other objects.

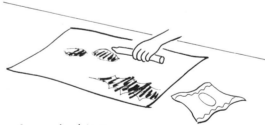

VARIATIONS

- Use a different color crayon for each object.
- Do a rubbing with items that are related (e.g., items all from nature, items all from the hardware store).
- Go on a walk with the children. Gather objects to use in crayon rubbings.
- Have the children bring in items from home to use in crayon rubbings.

NOTES FOR NEXT TIME: _____

_____

_____

_____

Basic Crayon Shavings

MATERIALS

- ☐ unwrapped crayons
- ☐ pencil sharpener
- ☐ glue
- ☐ paper

HELPFUL HINTS

- Children will enjoy shredding the crayons. It is also a good small motor exercise.
- This activity makes great use of broken crayons.

DEVELOPMENTAL GOALS

Develop creativity, small motor development, and hand-eye coordination and explore another use for crayons.

PREPARATION

Peel off the jackets of various colored crayons. The children enjoy doing this. Insert the crayons in a pencil sharpener to make shavings.

PROCESS

1. Spread glue over a sheet of paper.
2. Press the crayon shavings into an interesting design or picture.
3. Let the glue dry thoroughly.

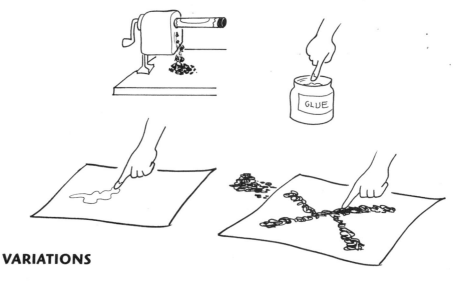

VARIATIONS

- Moisten the sticky side of a length of paper tape and glue the crayon shavings to the tape.
- Spread glue on parts of a crayon drawing and sprinkle crayon shavings on it for an interesting effect.

NOTES FOR NEXT TIME: _____

_____

_____

_____

Carton Creatures

MATERIALS

- ☐ recycled boxes
- ☐ cardboard rolls from paper towels or gift wrap
- ☐ collage materials
- ☐ construction paper
- ☐ markers
- ☐ glue
- ☐ blunt-tip scissors
- ☐ clean paper
- ☐ plastic milk cartons

HELPFUL HINTS

- While children are creating their animals, talk about the art elements you see in their work (e.g., line, shape, form, color, texture) and principles of visual organization (e.g., unity, variety, balance repetition/rhythm/pattern).
- Younger children (3 years and under) may tear the paper to fit the carton. Children 4 years and older may be better able to cut the paper with scissors.

DEVELOPMENTAL GOALS

Develop creativity, small motor development, and hand-eye coordination; encourage recycling and focus on art elements of line, shape, form, color, and texture.

PREPARATION

Discuss the animals the children would like to invent. Talk about the animal's size, shape, color, and texture.

PROCESS

1. Create an animal with milk cartons, cardboard tubes, and other materials.
2. Glue the animal together. Let it dry overnight.
3. If desired, cover the creature with construction paper.
4. Decorate it with markers.
5. Add cloth and trim scraps and any other collage materials for details.
6. Let the glue dry overnight.

VARIATIONS

- Make enough animals for a play zoo, farm, or pet store.
- Include the imaginary animals in the block or housekeeping area.
- Ask children which sounds their imaginary animals make. What do the animals eat? Where do they live? What is it like there?

NOTES FOR NEXT TIME: _____

_____

_____

_____

Chalk-Texture Experiences

MATERIALS

- ☐ thin paper (e.g., copy or tracing paper)
- ☐ sandpaper
- ☐ bricks
- ☐ corrugated cardboard
- ☐ chalk

HELPFUL HINT

- This is a good activity even for the very young artist because it involves simple hand movements.

DEVELOPMENTAL GOALS

Develop creativity, small motor development, and hand-eye coordination and explore new chalk experiences.

PREPARATION

Collect objects with interesting textures. Discuss the textures. Use words like *coarse*, *bumpy*, *rough*, and any other descriptive words.

PROCESS

1. Place thin paper over a surface with a unique texture.
2. Rub over the paper with the side of the chalk.
3. The texture of the object appears on the paper.
4. Use several objects for many interesting effects.

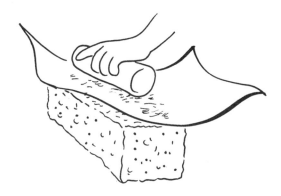

VARIATIONS

- Use a different color of chalk for each object.
- Add details with crayons or markers.
- Go outside and make chalk rubbings on the bark of trees, on the sidewalk, or on the grass.

NOTES FOR NEXT TIME: _____

_____

_____

_____

Chalk ABCs

MATERIALS

☐ sidewalk chalk in several colors

HELPFUL HINT

• This activity is appropriate for children who know the alphabet.

DEVELOPMENTAL GOALS

Develop creativity, small motor development, and hand-eye coordination and emphasize letter and number recognition and patterning.

PREPARATION

Have the children practice writing their names or some words before going outside for this activity. Give each letter of the alphabet a color. For example, the first letter A is red, the second letter B is blue, the third letter is yellow, the fourth letter is red (again), and so on. Make an alphabet chart showing the color sequence.

PROCESS

1. Take the children, color alphabet chart, and sidewalk chalk outside.
2. Have the children use colored chalk to write their names and words following the color chart.
3. Numbers can be any color the children want.
4. Let the children repeat the process as many times as time allows.

VARIATIONS

• Write spelling words outside using the color sequence.
• Do the same activity inside using chalk and paper.

NOTES FOR NEXT TIME: _____

_____

_____

_____

CRAYONS, CHALK, AND MARKERS

Chalk and Tempera Paint

MATERIALS

- ☐ chalk
- ☐ tempera paint
- ☐ shallow container for paint
- ☐ paper
- ☐ pencils

HELPFUL HINTS

- After the paint is dry, an adult sprays the drawing with hairspray. Be sure to spray in a well-ventilated area.
- This activity is suitable for children able to use pencils and chalk.

DEVELOPMENTAL GOALS

Develop creativity, small motor development, and hand-eye coordination and explore chalk and tempera technique.

PREPARATION

Discuss with the children which kind of pencil drawing or design they would like to make. Explain that they will be using tempera paint and chalk with this drawing.

PROCESS

1. Make a light pencil outline drawing on paper.
2. Mix tempera paint to the consistency of cream.
3. Dip the end of colored chalk into chosen color paint.
4. Apply paint with chalk stick in brush-like strokes.
5. Continue until the picture is completed.

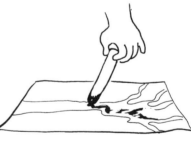

VARIATIONS

- Add details with plain chalk.
- Try light colors on dark paper and vice versa.

NOTES FOR NEXT TIME: _____

_____

_____

_____

Chalk and Tempera Print

MATERIALS

- ☐ colored chalk
- ☐ white tempera paint
- ☐ paper
- ☐ large brush

HELPFUL HINT

- Some children may lack the attention span for the two-step process. It is perfectly acceptable for these children to complete just one of the steps if they so choose.

DEVELOPMENTAL GOALS

Develop creativity, small motor development, and hand-eye coordination and explore chalk and tempera technique.

PREPARATION

Discuss with the children the kind of picture or design they would like to make. Explain that they will be making a print of this picture.

PROCESS

1. Make a design or drawing with colored chalk on a piece of good-quality paper. Be sure to use the chalk heavily.

2. Coat another piece of paper of the same size with white tempera paint

3. Use a large brush and paint in both directions to smooth the paint over one entire side of the paper.

4. While the tempera is still wet, place the chalk drawing face down in the tempera paint.

5. Rub firmly over the paper with the fingers and/or the hand.

6. Separate the two papers before they are dry.

7. Two prints will result—the chalk will have merged with the paint on both prints.

VARIATION

- Experiment with different colors of chalk and tempera paint to produce many interesting effects.

NOTES FOR NEXT TIME: _____

_____

_____

_____

CRAYONS, CHALK, AND MARKERS

Chalk Body Tracing

MATERIALS

☐ outdoor chalk (extra-large chalk)

☐ concrete area for chalk drawing

HELPFUL HINTS

• This is a great activity for a sunny, warm day, but it could also be done on a cooler day when the children are wearing jackets. Note how different these body outlines are from those on a sunny day.

• This activity can be used with toddlers as they can scribble inside, outside, or anywhere near their body outlines. Details are unneeded for this age group.

DEVELOPMENTAL GOALS

Develop creativity, small motor development, and hand-eye coordination and explore the outdoor use of chalk.

PREPARATION

Check out a concrete area that is appropriate for chalk drawings.

PROCESS

1. Have a child lie down face-up on the cement.
2. Have another child or an adult trace around the child's body with chalk.
3. Have the child color in the body outline.
4. Add details such as clothing, hair and eye color, and so on.

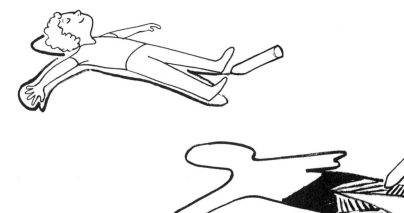

VARIATIONS

• Let the children color and add detail to each others' chalk body outlines.
• Write descriptive words or statements near the outline, as dictated by the child. This is a good way to tie language arts to this activity.

NOTES FOR NEXT TIME: _____

_____

_____

_____

All Ages

Chalk-Sand Painting

DEVELOPMENTAL GOALS

Develop creativity, small motor development, and hand-eye coordination and explore more chalk techniques.

MATERIALS

- ☐ sawdust or sand
- ☐ old pieces of broken chalk
- ☐ dry tempera paint
- ☐ water
- ☐ bowl
- ☐ construction paper
- ☐ glue

PREPARATION

Shave chalk with a knife (adults only). Put sawdust or sand with chalk shavings mixed with tempera paint (dry) in a bowl of water (just enough water to cover). Stir and allow to dry overnight. This will make a colorful sand (or sawdust) material.

PROCESS

1. Apply glue or paste to a piece of construction paper.
2. Sprinkle colored sand or sawdust over the glued area to create a sand painting.

HELPFUL HINT

- Even the youngest artists will enjoy sprinkling this colorful sand on the glue-covered paper. They probably will enjoy spreading on the glue just as much!

VARIATIONS

- Outline the details of the picture with crayons or markers.
- Make a sand painting on posterboard or cardboard.

NOTES FOR NEXT TIME: _____

_____

_____

_____

Chalk Shape Rubbings

All Ages

MATERIALS

- ☐ chalk
- ☐ thin paper (e.g., copy paper)
- ☐ scissors
- ☐ shapes cut out of sandpaper
- ☐ pieces of screen
- ☐ corrugated cardboard
- ☐ any other materials with obvious texture

HELPFUL HINTS

- This is a good activity for encouraging vocabulary development by talking about shapes, size, number, and so on.
- With toddlers, use only one or two shapes for this activity.

DEVELOPMENTAL GOALS

Develop creativity, small motor development, and hand-eye coordination and reinforce shapes, sizes, and object placement.

PREPARATION

Discuss shapes with the children. Talk about how shapes are all around, such as in round plates, rectangular books, and triangular blocks. Allow children to choose a shape.

PROCESS

1. Place paper over the shape.
2. Make a chalk rubbing of the shape with the side of the chalk.
3. Choose another shape.
4. Make another chalk rubbing of this shape.
5. Continue until satisfied with the design.

VARIATIONS

- Use other flat shapes, such as puzzle or game pieces, buttons, or parquetry blocks for chalk rubbings.
- Let the children find interesting shapes for chalk rubbings.
- Do chalk rubbings of numbers and letters cut out of sandpaper or other textured materials.

NOTES FOR NEXT TIME: _____

_____

_____

Chalk Stenciling

MATERIALS

- ☐ drawing paper
- ☐ scissors
- ☐ facial tissue
- ☐ small piece of cotton or patch of cloth
- ☐ colored chalk

HELPFUL HINTS

- This activity is appropriate for children who can use scissors.
- When rubbing with tissue, it works best to make strokes from the stencil paper toward the center of the opening. Continue this around the edge of the opening until the paper under the stencil has a clear print.

DEVELOPMENTAL GOALS

Develop creativity, small motor development, and hand-eye coordination and explore a new chalking technique.

PREPARATION

Cut the drawing paper into pieces about 4" square. Give each child four or five pieces of paper.

PROCESS

1. With scissors, cut holes or shapes of various sizes and shapes in the center of each piece. This is the stencil.
2. Cut more than one hole or shape in each piece for more interesting stencils.
3. Rub a piece of tissue, a small piece of cotton, or a patch of cloth over a piece of colored chalk.
4. Rub the tissue, cotton, or patch of cloth until it picks up enough dust to make a stencil.
5. Place the cut-out stencil over another piece of paper.
6. Rub the chalk dust over the stencil, covering the entire shape with chalk dust.
7. Continue using the same stencil again over the paper or use another stencil.

VARIATIONS

- Use a combination of several stencils on one piece of paper for visual rhythms.
- Cut stencils of objects, such as trees, ornaments, and animals.
- Holiday cards, programs, and decorations may be made from stencils.
- The same technique can be used with wax crayons.

NOTES FOR NEXT TIME: _____

_____

Chalk, Tempera, and Starch Print

MATERIALS

- ☐ liquid starch
- ☐ powdered tempera paint
- ☐ brushes
- ☐ a scratching instrument (e.g., a stick, a spoon)
- ☐ colored chalk
- ☐ two sheets of paper per child

HELPFUL HINTS

- Young artists who have had experience painting with a brush should be able to enjoy this activity.
- Liquid starch is available in the grocery store where laundry products are sold.

DEVELOPMENTAL GOALS

Develop creativity, small motor development, and hand-eye coordination and explore the use of chalk in printing.

PREPARATION

Mix the liquid starch and tempera paint to produce a dripless paint.

PROCESS

1. Brush the paint and starch mixture on a sheet of paper.
2. Scratch a design in the wet paint.
3. Coat another sheet of paper with colored chalk.
4. Place the second sheet, chalk side down, over the wet paint surface.
5. Lightly rub the back of the top sheet.
6. Pull off the top sheet.

VARIATIONS

- Use different kinds of paper and colors.
- After the prints are dry, add details with crayons and markers.
- These prints make attractive wrapping paper.
- Cover the prints with clear Contac® paper and use them for placemats.

NOTES FOR NEXT TIME: _____

_____

_____

Crayons and Wax-Paper Creations

3 Years Old and UP

MATERIALS

- ☐ autumn leaves or other natural objects (e.g., dried weeds or flowers)
- ☐ wax paper
- ☐ crayon shavings
- ☐ iron
- ☐ pieces of cardboard (to press on)

HELPFUL HINTS

- Be very careful when using an iron around the children! Caution the children to stay well away from the iron during the pressing.
- This activity can be used with many other themes by using cut-out construction paper objects. For example, a Valentine's Day theme would involve cut-out paper hearts and crayon shavings. A birthday theme could be cut-out paper candles and cake and crayon shavings. A "Me" theme could include cut-out magazine pictures of favorite things with crayon shavings scattered for effect.

DEVELOPMENTAL GOALS

Develop creativity, small motor development, and hand-eye coordination and explore a different use for crayon shavings.

PREPARATION

Go on a walk to collect interesting natural objects for this activity. Have the children choose their favorite leaves, flowers, or weeds for their original creations. Shave crayons by putting them through a pencil sharpener.

PROCESS

1. Place leaves, weeds, or dried flowers on a sheet of waxed paper.
2. Arrange and rearrange the items until satisfied with the design.
3. Sprinkle crayon shavings around the arrangement.
4. Place another piece of waxed paper on top.
5. The adult presses with a warm iron, sealing the artwork between the pieces of waxed paper.

VARIATIONS

- If leaves are not available, cut leaf shapes from colored construction paper.
- Use several colors of crayon shavings.
- Hang these nature pictures on a window. The light will shine through them.
- These nature pictures also make nice placemats.

NOTES FOR NEXT TIME:

_____

_____

Crayon Batik

3 Years Old and Up

MATERIALS

- ☐ crayons
- ☐ paper
- ☐ water
- ☐ container for water
- ☐ thin solution of tempera paint
- ☐ brushes
- ☐ paper towels

HELPFUL HINTS

- Because the color will be more intense in the creased area, the finished drawing will have dramatic contrasts.
- This activity is appropriate for children who have lots of experience using crayons.
- Bring in some samples of batik fabric for the children to see. These can be found in most fabric stores in the cotton-fabric section. Many ethnic fabrics are also made with batik designs.

DEVELOPMENTAL GOALS

Develop creativity, small motor development, and hand-eye coordination and explore a new crayoning technique.

PREPARATION

Discuss that the term *batik* is a design with wrinkles in the paper. This is part of the design. Talk about which kind of picture or design the children would like to make in this activity.

PROCESS

1. Make a drawing or design with the crayons on paper.
2. Soak the paper in water.
3. Crumple the paper into a ball.
4. Uncrumple the paper.
5. Flatten it.
6. Blot off excess water with paper towels.
7. Flow diluted tempera paint over the surface with a wet brush.
8. Let the batik dry thoroughly.

VARIATIONS

- Draw with light-colored crayons and cover the drawing with dark tempera paint.
- Draw with dark-colored crayons and cover the drawing with light tempera paint.
- After the painting has dried, add more design elements or details with markers.

NOTES FOR NEXT TIME: _____

_____

_____

Crayon Cupcakes

MATERIALS

- ☐ broken crayons of various sizes and colors
- ☐ muffin tins
- ☐ oven

HELPFUL HINTS

- Adult super-vision is always required when working around an oven.

- Let the children unwrap the crayons. They love to do it, and it is great exer-cise for the small muscles in the fingers and hands.

DEVELOPMENTAL GOALS

Develop creativity, small motor development, and hand-eye coordination and encourage crayon recycling.

PREPARATION

Unwrap all crayons.

PROCESS

1. Sort the crayons by color.
2. Fill the muffin tins loosely with different colors.
3. Mix colors, if desired. Try white and red for pink, for example.
4. Put the filled muffin tins in a 250 degree oven for about 20 minutes.
5. Let the tins cool completely after baking.
6. Place the tins in the refrigerator, or put them outside if it is cool.
7. Pop the cupcakes out, and they are ready to go.

VARIATIONS

- Put several colors of crayons in one muffin tin cup. See how it comes out!
- Sprinkle in some glitter with the crayons before baking to create a sparkly recycled crayon!
- Mix primary colors. See what happens!

NOTES FOR NEXT TIME: _____

_____

_____

CRAYONS, CHALK, AND MARKERS 15

A
All Ages

Crayon Explorations

MATERIALS

- ☐ crayons
- ☐ construction paper
- ☐ chalk
- ☐ various surfaces (see the following)

HELPFUL HINT

- Be open to all suggestions. Children may come up with some amazing and funny suggestions.

DEVELOPMENTAL GOALS

Develop creativity, small motor development, and hand-eye coordination and explore different crayoning techniques.

PREPARATION

Collect corrugated cardboard, cloth, wood, paper rolls, sandpaper, and other interesting items for crayoning activities.

PROCESS

1. Encourage the children to explore the various items and to choose one or two for crayoning.
2. Challenge the children to use crayon and white chalk on colored construction paper.
3. Try drawing or scribbling with crayons on cardboard or sandpaper.
4. Consider drawing or scribbling with crayons on pieces of wood.
5. Find out how crayons work on pieces of cloth.

VARIATIONS

- Let the children come up with new and different surfaces for their crayon drawings.
- Keep examples of some of these crayon explorations to help you and the children remember them for next time.

NOTES FOR NEXT TIME: _____

_____

_____

_____

Crayon Feeling Pictures

All Ages

MATERIALS

☐ crayons
☐ paper

HELPFUL HINT

- This activity is appropriate for even the youngest child, because it is free-form and encourages spontaneous drawing.

NOTES FOR NEXT TIME:

_____

_____

_____

_____

_____

_____

DEVELOPMENTAL GOALS

Develop creativity, small motor development, and hand-eye coordination and express feelings through crayoning.

PREPARATION

Discuss the variety of lines with the children. Use words like *fat, wavy, textured, thin,* and *zig-zag*.

PROCESS

1. The adult takes a crayon and draws randomly on the paper while describing a feeling the adult had that morning (e.g., "First, I got out of bed" while drawing a line that shows the movement getting out of bed).

2. "Then I went to the shower" while making scribble lines to mimic water falling.

3. "Then I dried myself off with a fluffy towel" while making zig-zag lines to mimic the movement of the towel.

4. Have the children do their own feeling drawings, going through what they did in the morning or throughout the day.

5. Encourage the children to fill the page with lines showing their activities.

6. Encourage the children to change colors frequently.

7. Use the crayon on the side to make fat lines.

VARIATIONS

- The more motion, the better. The more variety of line, the better.
- Fill spaces between lines with crayons or markers.
- Let the children tell about their feelings while pointing to the lines they made on the page.

Crayon Leaf Designs

MATERIALS

- ☐ crayons
- ☐ paper
- ☐ a variety of leaves

HELPFUL HINT

- Go on a walk outdoors and collect the leaves for this activity.

DEVELOPMENTAL GOALS

Develop creativity, small motor development, and hand-eye coordination and develop an appreciation for lines and shapes in nature.

PREPARATION

Unwrap the crayons so they can be used on their sides as well as on their tips. Discuss with the children the lines, shapes, sizes, and details of the leaves collected for this activity. Use such words as *vertical*, *horizontal* and even *swerved* when discussing the types of lines seen in the leaves.

PROCESS

1. On a sheet of paper, arrange the leaves in a design.
2. When satisfied with the design, cover it with a thin sheet of paper.
3. Rub over the paper with crayon.
4. Make an overall design by moving the objects several times and repeating the rubbing.

VARIATIONS

- Colors may be overlapped and blended to create interesting effects.
- Add details to the leaf rubbing with colored markers or crayons.
- Older children may want to label the leaves on their designs. They could look them up in an encyclopedia (book or even online!) to help identify each leaf.

NOTES FOR NEXT TIME: _____

_____

_____

_____

4

Crayon over Tempera Paint

MATERIALS

- ☐ tempera paints and brushes
- ☐ wax crayons
- ☐ paper
- ☐ sponge
- ☐ water
- ☐ container for water

HELPFUL HINTS

- The degree of flaking may be sped up by brushing or, if it has gone too far, retouching may be done with the crayons.

- This is an excellent activity for older children who think using crayons is "boring."

DEVELOPMENTAL GOALS

Develop creativity, small motor development, and hand-eye coordination and explore a new crayoning technique.

PREPARATION

Children make pictures or designs of their choice with tempera paint on paper. Let the pictures dry thoroughly.

PROCESS

1. Work a contrasting color crayon over each area, using moderate pressure.

2. Immerse the sponge in water.

3. "Wash" the painting until the underlying tempera paint begins flaking off.

4. The result will be a picture of mottled, textured quality. The crayon left on will accent the varied tempera tones that remain.

VARIATION

- This technique may be modified by applying the crayons more heavily, then holding the drawing under water that is just hot enough to melt the crayons. Be very careful if you choose this variation. The teacher should hold the drawing under the hot water.

NOTES FOR NEXT TIME: _____

_____

_____

Crayon Resist

MATERIALS

- ☐ wax crayons
- ☐ paper
- ☐ brush
- ☐ tempera paint
- ☐ water container

HELPFUL HINT

- Be sure the mixture of tempera paint is thin. A too-thick mix will darken too much of the crayon drawing.

DEVELOPMENTAL GOALS

Develop creativity, small motor development, and hand-eye coordination and explore a new crayoning technique.

PREPARATION

Discuss with the children the designs or pictures they might like to make for this activity. Explain that the design will be covered with paint and will look different when painted over.

PROCESS

1. Make a design or picture with crayons. Press very hard with the crayon to make it thick on the paper.
2. Leave some areas of the paper uncolored.
3. Cover the entire surface of the paper with tempera paint.
4. The paint will be absorbed by the uncolored paper.
5. The paint will be "resisted" by the wax crayons.

VARIATIONS

- Use light-colored or white crayons with dark tempera paint for an interesting effect.
- Crayon resist can make dramatic effects in special holiday pictures.
- Instead of crayons, use a candle stub to draw a picture. Then, paint over the design with thin tempera paint.

NOTES FOR NEXT TIME: _____

_____

_____

_____

Crayon-Rubbing Pictures

MATERIALS

- ☐ crayons
- ☐ textured surfaces (e.g., sandpaper, pieces of screen, cardboard)
- ☐ newsprint or another thin-type paper

HELPFUL HINT

- This activity is appropriate for children who are already using crayons.

DEVELOPMENTAL GOALS

Develop creativity, small motor development, and hand-eye coordination and explore a new approach to crayon rubbing.

PREPARATION

Discuss the pieces of textured surfaces with the children. Use descriptive words like *coarse*, *bumpy*, and *criss-cross*.

PROCESS

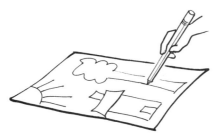

1. Make an outline drawing with a pencil on thin paper.
2. Hold the drawing against a surface that has a definite texture.
3. Rub the crayon over all areas of the drawing, filling the area with an interesting texture pattern.
4. The texture will transfer to the paper.
5. Place the paper against another texture and transfer this texture to another part of the drawing.
6. Textures may be repeated or overlapped.
7. Continue until all areas are filled with texture rubbings.

VARIATIONS

- Unusual effects can be obtained by using several colors of crayons.
- Make the outline drawing in crayon and markers. Do the rubbings for texture effects on them.

NOTES FOR NEXT TIME: _____

_____

_____

_____

Crayon Scratchings

MATERIALS

- ☐ paper
- ☐ crayons
- ☐ black tempera paint
- ☐ a drop of liquid soap (dishwashing liquid soap)
- ☐ paintbrush
- ☐ paper clips

HELPFUL HINT

- This activity is appropriate for children who have a lot of experience using crayons.

DEVELOPMENTAL GOALS

Develop creativity, small motor development, and hand-eye coordination and explore a new crayoning technique.

PREPARATION

Give each child a piece of heavy paper. Manila paper works well for this activity.

PROCESS

1. Color a sheet of paper with bright crayons.
2. Make stripes, blotches, or any pattern.
3. Press hard to make a thick layer of crayon all over the paper.
4. Paint a coat of black tempera paint all over the top of the crayon.
5. Add a drop of liquid soap to the black paint so it will stick to crayon wax.
6. Let the paint dry thoroughly.
7. Scratch a design or picture into the black surface with a bent paper clip. The bright crayon color will show beautifully through the black.

VARIATIONS

- Scratch letters or numbers into the crayon.
- Make a group scratch project. Use a large piece of paper and divide it up for each student to fill with crayon. Make a group decision about what to scratch into the crayon.

NOTES FOR NEXT TIME: _____

_____

_____

_____

Crayon Shavings– The Hot Way!

4 Years Old and UP

MATERIALS

- ☐ old electric iron
- ☐ heavy cardboard box close to size of the iron
- ☐ old, broken wax crayons
- ☐ paper
- ☐ cardboard
- ☐ pencil sharpener
- ☐ tape

HELPFUL HINTS

- Be very careful when using an iron around the children. Be sure the children maintain a safe distance from it. An adult should always be the one to handle the iron.
- Heat sources other than the iron may be used to melt the shavings. The drawing may be placed in direct sunlight, on a radiator, or over a lightbulb. Take care to avoid too much exposure, which will make the wax run.

DEVELOPMENTAL GOALS

Develop creativity, small motor development, and hand-eye coordination and explore a new crayon-shaving use.

PREPARATION

Shave the wax crayons in the pencil sharpener. The adult must place the iron in the cardboard box with the ironing surface up. Plug in and turn on the iron to the "low" setting.

PROCESS

1. Tape the edges of the paper to a piece of cardboard.
2. Drop some crayon shavings onto the paper.
3. Push the shavings around until the design or picture is created.
4. Pass the paper above the heated iron until the crayon shavings begin to melt. (Supervise closely.)
5. Continue this process with additional crayon until the desired pattern is created.

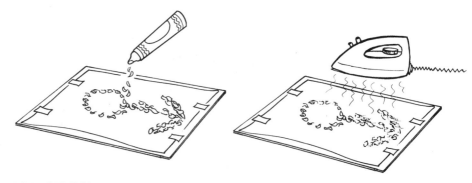

VARIATION

- Add details to the picture or design with tempera paint, crayons, or markers.

NOTES FOR NEXT TIME: _____

_____

_____

_____

Crayon-Transfer Print

MATERIALS

- ☐ paper
- ☐ colored chalk
- ☐ crayons
- ☐ pencil or ball-point pen

HELPFUL HINTS

- Some children may lack the attention span to complete the two-step process. Allow these children to complete just one step.

- The simpler the drawing or the design, the better the results with the crayon-transfer print.

- You may want to introduce the words *positive* and *reverse* when doing the crayon-transfer print.

DEVELOPMENTAL GOALS

Develop creativity, small motor development, and hand-eye coordination and explore a new crayoning technique.

PREPARATION

Discuss with the children which kind of design or picture they would like to make. Explain that the children will be making more than one copy of this artwork by making a "transfer print."

PROCESS

1. Completely cover a sheet of white paper with a heavy coating of light-colored chalk.

2. Cover the coating of chalk with a very heavy layer of darker colored crayon.

3. Make a design or drawing on another piece of white paper.

4. Place the drawing over the crayon and chalk-covered paper.

5. Using a dull pencil or ball-point pen and using pressure, trace over the drawing.

6. The pressure causes the crayon to adhere to the underside of the drawing. It creates a separate drawing on the crayon and chalk-covered paper.

VARIATION

- Use different colors of chalk and crayons and repeat this activity.

NOTES FOR NEXT TIME: _____

_____

_____

Disappearing Line Drawings

MATERIALS

☐ hard soap (the type from hotels works well)

☐ black construction paper

☐ crayons

☐ water

☐ sink or large tub of water

HELPFUL HINT

• Through this activity children should see how important lines are to a drawing. Some lines outline shapes or forms and can still be seen, but, in many cases, the lines are the artwork.

DEVELOPMENTAL GOALS

Develop creativity, small motor development, and hand-eye coordination and appreciate the importance of lines in drawings.

PREPARATION

Talk about lines in drawings and how they can be straight, curvy, horizontal, vertical, zigzag, and so on. This project is messy, so you may want rubber gloves and a newspaper-covered drying area.

PROCESS

1. Give each child a piece of black paper.
2. Do a line drawing with the soap.
3. The drawing should have lots of outlined areas in which to color.
4. Note that the soap will not work for areas the children want white; for these areas the children must use white crayon.
5. Color in the drawing. Light colors work best.
6. Rinse the drawing until the soap lines disappear.
7. Allow to dry.

VARIATION

• Draw a design using only shapes. Repeat the process.

NOTES FOR NEXT TIME: _____

_____

_____

Fantastic Plants

MATERIALS

- ☐ scissors
- ☐ crayons
- ☐ glue
- ☐ construction paper
- ☐ scrap pieces of trim and fabric

HELPFUL HINT

- Children aged 3 and younger may be most interested exploring glue texture in this activity. This is appropriate, because they are learning how these materials work.

DEVELOPMENTAL GOALS

Develop creativity, small motor development, and hand-eye coordination and tie science to art activities.

PREPARATION

Talk with the children about plants. Observe the plants outdoors. Discuss the differences in stems, bark, leaves, flowers, and other plant parts.

PROCESS

1. Choose a favorite plant, such as a fruit tree, a pine tree, or a prickly cactus.
2. Think about how special you can make this plant.
3. Create the plant with crayons.
4. Glue on cut-out construction pieces for details.
5. Add pieces of trim or fabric scraps for more detail.

VARIATIONS

- Make crayon rubbings of tree bark or dried leaves. Cut out the rubbings and include them in the plant picture.
- Glue on real leaves and twigs for details.
- Do this activity outdoors with nature all around for inspiration!
- Create imaginary plants with fantastic colors and details.

NOTES FOR NEXT TIME: _____

_____

_____

_____

First Chalk Experiences

MATERIALS

- ☐ fat, soft chalk of different colors
- ☐ brown paper bag
- ☐ water
- ☐ container for water

HELPFUL HINT

- Cover each piece of chalk with a piece of aluminum foil, leaving about half an inch of the chalk exposed. This prevents smearing colors on the hands and fingers. It also prevents the transferring of colors from one piece of chalk to another while they are stored.

DEVELOPMENTAL GOALS

Develop creativity, small motor development, and hand-eye coordination and introduce the medium of chalk.

PREPARATION

Cut open the brown paper bags so they are flat.

PROCESS

1. Dip the brown paper in water.
2. Draw with dry chalk on the wet brown paper.
3. Colors will be bright and almost fluorescent.

VARIATIONS

- Use white or manila paper and repeat the process.
- Try using light colors of chalk on dark paper and dark chalk on light paper.

NOTES FOR NEXT TIME: _____

_____

_____

_____

Line Dancing

DEVELOPMENTAL GOALS

Develop creativity, small motor development, and hand-eye coordination and explore line and movement to tie music to art.

MATERIALS

- ☐ a variety of instruments (e.g., rattles, drums, bells, kazoos, re- corders, tambourines)
- ☐ paper
- ☐ markers

HELPFUL HINT

- There is no single or right answer to the kind of lines that go with each instrument. A child may make one line for a tri- angle on the first hearing and another type of line the next time it is played. In that way, music is very much like art.

PREPARATION

Discuss the instruments gathered for this activity. Let the children hold, touch, and use them. Talk about the sounds each makes.

PROCESS

1. Play one of the instruments.
2. Talk about the kind of line the instrument sounds like. For example, a triangle can be a dotted line, a kazoo a straight line, or a tam- bourine zigzag lines.
3. Draw a line for each of the instrument's sounds.
4. Keep playing the instruments to see if new lines come to mind for the sound.
5. Fill the paper with different kinds of lines for the various instruments.

VARIATIONS

- Decide which type of movement goes with the lines (e.g., a sliding step for a straight line, hopping on one foot for a dotted line, waving your arms for a wavy line). Have fun acting out these lines!
- Play "Simon Says" using the steps above for the commands. For example, "Simon Says to be a dotted line." The children would hop on one foot to be a dotted line.
- Play classical, pop, or any other type of music. Have the children draw lines to go with the music. For example, in fast parts of the music, make spiral lines. In the slower parts, make slow, curvy lines. Fill the paper with lines representing the piece of music.

NOTES FOR NEXT TIME: _____

_____

_____

Markers and Wet Paper

MATERIALS

- ☐ paper
- ☐ markers
- ☐ brush
- ☐ water
- ☐ container for water

HELPFUL HINT

- Use watercolor markers, not permanent markers, for this activity.

DEVELOPMENTAL GOALS

Develop creativity, small motor development, and hand-eye coordination and explore a new technique with colored markers.

PREPARATION

Paint an entire sheet of paper with water.

PROCESS

1. While paper is still wet, draw on it with markers.
2. Watch the colors run.
3. See how the shapes and lines soften.

VARIATION

- Draw with marker, then squirt with water. You will get the same softening and running of colors.

NOTES FOR NEXT TIME: _____

_____

_____

Outdoor Chalk Fun

MATERIALS

- ☐ sidewalk chalk (extra-large chalk)
- ☐ toy cars, trucks, trains

HELPFUL HINT

- Be sure you check that it is all right to draw on the concrete area before starting this activity!

DEVELOPMENTAL GOALS

Develop creativity, small motor development, and hand-eye coordination and explore a new chalk technique.

PREPARATION

Talk about the toy vehicles and where they can be found. Discuss the neighborhood and where the cars, trucks, and trains are found.

PROCESS

1. Go outside and choose a concrete area for chalk drawings.
2. Let the children draw roads for the toy vehicles.
3. Draw buildings and houses.
4. Include people, pets, trees, and other details.

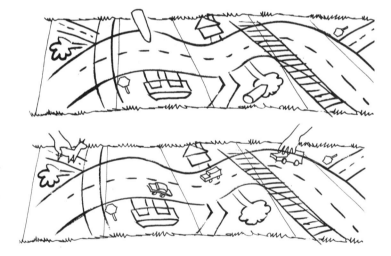

VARIATION

- Use a long piece of paper (butcher paper is a good choice) to repeat this activity indoors. Draw the roads, houses, buildings, and so on on the paper with chalk, crayons, or markers.

NOTES FOR NEXT TIME: _____

_____

_____

_____

Paper Quilts

MATERIALS

- ☐ blunt-tip scissors
- ☐ markers
- ☐ construction paper
- ☐ white paper
- ☐ glue
- ☐ glitter (optional)
- ☐ wallpaper samples

HELPFUL HINTS

- Cut a square template out of sturdy paper (gift box material or even cardboard). This will help the children make their squares. The children simply trace around the template onto the wallpaper with a crayon or pencil. Then, they can simply cut along these lines.
- You may have to precut the squares for children not yet able to use scissors.

DEVELOPMENTAL GOALS

Develop creativity, small motor development, and hand-eye coordination and explore a new use for markers to reinforce the design elements of rhythm, repetition unity, balance, and pattern.

PREPARATION

Find quilts or books with pictures of quilts made with square patches. Discuss the patterns in the quilts. Talk about the rhythm or repetition of certain lines in the quilts. Discuss the shapes the children see in the quilts. Talk about how the square patches are put together to make a harmonious design or pattern.

PROCESS

1. Choose several pieces of wallpaper.
2. Cut squares out of the wallpaper.
3. Arrange the wallpaper squares on a piece of white paper.
4. When satisfied with the arrangement, glue the pieces to the paper.
5. Use markers to outline areas of interest.

VARIATIONS

- Put the children's quilts together to make a class quilt.
- Read stories about quilt making in several cultures.
- Ask a family member to demonstrate quilting. Watch the quilter at work.

NOTES FOR NEXT TIME: _____
_____
_____
_____

Years Old and UP

Poetry and Chalk Art

MATERIALS

☐ white and pastel colored chalk

☐ dark construction paper

HELPFUL HINT

• If some children have trouble seeing mind pictures, ask them to draw a picture of the season. Anything they want to draw is acceptable.

DEVELOPMENTAL GOALS

Develop creativity, small motor development, and hand-eye coordination and encourage the appreciation of poetry that ties art and language arts.

PREPARATION

Read the poem "Snowstorm" to the children once.

Snowstorm

I love to see the snowflakes fall,
And cover everything in sight.
The lawn and trees and orchard wall
With spotless white.

PROCESS

1. Ask what the children saw in their minds when they heard the poem.

2. Read the poem again, and ask how many childen saw pictures of the scene in their minds.

3. Have a discussion. Let the children share their mind pictures of the poem.

4. Give each child a piece of dark construction paper.

5. With white and pastel chalk, have the children draw what comes to mind when they hear the poem.

VARIATIONS

• Use other poems about different seasons.

• Use a CD or tape of classical, rock, or other kinds of music. Ask the children to draw mind pictures of the music.

NOTES FOR NEXT TIME: _____

_____

_____

_____

Pressed-Plant Designs

MATERIALS

- ☐ cardboard
- ☐ construction paper
- ☐ recycled newspapers
- ☐ leaves
- ☐ flowers
- ☐ markers
- ☐ glue
- ☐ paper towels

HELPFUL HINT

- Very young children will have a hard time waiting for the plants and flowers to dry. It may help to let them peek every day to see how it is going.

NOTES FOR NEXT TIME:

_____
_____
_____
_____
_____
_____

DEVELOPMENTAL GOALS

Develop creativity, small motor development, and hand-eye coordination and tie science to art activities.

PREPARATION

On an outdoor walk, collect fallen leaves and flowers. Cut cardboard into two pieces approximately 12" × 18". Each child will need two pieces of cardboard.

PROCESS

1. Collect nonpoisonous fallen leaves and such flowers as dandelions or clover.

2. Make a plant press. On top of cardboard, layer two or three paper towels. Spread leaves or flowers flat on the paper towels.

3. Place several sheets of newspaper over the leaves or flowers.

4. Have a child write his or her name with markers on the newspaper. (An adult may do this for younger children.)

5. Put heavy books or bricks on the plant press. Dry the press overnight.

6. Change the newspaper each day until the plants/flowers are dry.

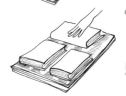

7. Arrange the dried plant on construction paper in a design.

8. Glue on cut-out pieces of construction paper for details.

9. Complete the design with markers for decorative details.

VARIATIONS

- Have the children predict what they think will happen to the color and shape of plants as they dry. Measure sizes. Draw before and after pictures.

- Talk about other dried things, like raisins, prunes, and apricots. Have these dried fruits available to taste.

- Mix dried milk. Try making gelatin or pudding as another example of a dried food.

Rubbing Chalk Experiences

MATERIALS

- ☐ chalk in many colors
- ☐ cotton swabs
- ☐ cotton balls
- ☐ paper

HELPFUL HINT

- This activity is appropriate for children who have had some experience using chalk.

DEVELOPMENTAL GOALS

Develop creativity, small motor development, and hand-eye coordination and explore new chalk techniques.

PREPARATION

Give the children a chance to experience using chalk on different kinds of papers. Note if some apply chalk in separate strokes. See if some blend the colors. Encourage the children to talk about their work with chalk.

PROCESS

1. Draw a picture or make a design with the chalk on paper.
2. Use a cotton swab or cotton ball to rub the chalk drawing to soften and blend the colors.
3. Expect that some colors may get muddied. This is a natural part of the process.

VARIATIONS

- Use different textures of paper.
- Use scraps of cloth for blending.
- Rub only certain sections of the picture or design. Talk about the differences.

NOTES FOR NEXT TIME: _____

_____

_____

_____

Salty Crayon Fun

MATERIALS

- ☐ dark construction paper
- ☐ crayons
- ☐ container for water
- ☐ salt
- ☐ brush
- ☐ water

HELPFUL HINT

- Be prepared for a bit more of a mess when you mix glitter into the thinned white glue. Considering the sparkly effects of this mixture, it is worth the mess!

DEVELOPMENTAL GOALS

Develop creativity, small motor development, and hand-eye coordination and explore a new use for crayons.

PREPARATION

Mix the salt and water, using twice the amount of salt as water (e.g., 2 cups salt to 1 cup water).

PROCESS

1. Draw with crayons on dark construction paper.
2. Paint the entire picture or design with the salt and water mixture.
3. When the water dries, the picture will sparkle.

VARIATIONS

- Thin white glue with water. Mix in glitter. Paint this mixture over a crayon drawing on light-colored construction paper. It will be another sparkly drawing!
- Make greeting cards and wrapping paper using this crayon technique.

NOTES FOR NEXT TIME: _____

_____

_____

_____

Sandy Chalk Work

MATERIALS

☐ colored chalk

☐ sandpaper (rough grade)

HELPFUL HINTS

- Spray the drawing with hairspray to help keep it from smearing. Be sure to spray in a well-ventilated area.

- This activity is appropriate for even the very young artist who is in the controlled scribble stage.

DEVELOPMENTAL GOALS

Develop creativity, small motor development, and hand-eye coordination and explore another chalking technique.

PREPARATION

Cover the ends of chalk with foil. This helps make them easier to hold when working on rough surfaces.

PROCESS

1. Draw with chalk on the sandpaper.

2. The rough surface of the sandpaper helps make rich and vivid texture effects.

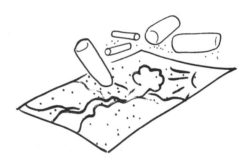

VARIATIONS

- Richer color can be achieved if the sandpaper is moist. It will also attract and hold greater amounts of rich chalk color.

- Use other grades of sandpaper for different effects.

NOTES FOR NEXT TIME: _____

_____

_____

_____

4 Years Old and Up

Scribbles

MATERIALS

- ☐ crayons
- ☐ paper
- ☐ markers

HELPFUL HINT

- This activity can be adapted to the very young artist and for the most "grown-up" one, as well. The younger the artist, the simpler the scribble activity. Older children will enjoy trying some of the variations.

DEVELOPMENTAL GOALS

Develop creativity, small motor development, and hand-eye coordination and explore a new crayoning technique.

PREPARATION

Discuss scribbling, how it looks, and how much fun it is to do. Explain that this activity begins with scribbling.

PROCESS

1. Make a large scribble on the paper.
2. Outline with a marker parts of the scribble.
3. Fill the outline areas with crayons.
4. Leave some areas uncolored.

VARIATIONS

- Make rules for filling the scribbles (e.g., "You can't put the same colors next to each other," "You can only use primary colors," "Use only complementary colors.").
- Challenge the children to make scribbles using straight lines and angles.
- Have a group of children make a scribble picture mural.
- Scribble using crayon, then paint the spaces using tempera paint.

NOTES FOR NEXT TIME: _____

_____

_____

_____

Shading with Chalk Dust

MATERIALS

- ☐ chalk
- ☐ flat, hard tool for scraping chalk into dust (e.g., knife, screwdriver)
- ☐ paper
- ☐ cotton balls
- ☐ facial tissue
- ☐ cotton swabs

HELPFUL HINTS

- Chalk is easily smeared and the completed drawing should have some protection. An adult may use hairspray for a fixative. Be sure to use it in a well-ventilated area.

- This activity requires experience with chalk drawing.

DEVELOPMENTAL GOALS

Develop creativity, small motor development, and hand-eye coordination and explore chalk as an expressive technique.

PREPARATION

An adult scrapes the tool along the side of the chalk to produce chalk dust. Collect the chalk dust in a jar lid or another small, shallow container.

PROCESS

1. Discuss shadows, light, and dark.
2. Talk about how chalk can be rubbed into drawings to make shadows or to make things look softer.
3. Make a chalk, crayon, or marker drawing/design.
4. Use the fingers or a cotton swab to sprinkle chalk dust into areas of a drawing or design.
5. Use tissue or a cotton ball to blend the dust in to make shadows and soft areas of color.

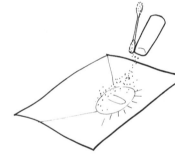

VARIATION

- The dust particles from the chalk may be scraped by the adult directly onto areas of the drawing.

NOTES FOR NEXT TIME: _____

_____

_____

_____

Shape Game

MATERIALS

- ☐ markers
- ☐ construction paper
- ☐ music
- ☐ music player
- ☐ ruler
- ☐ blunt scissors
- ☐ double-stick tape

HELPFUL HINTS

- Children under age 4 will need help cutting out the shape.
- The younger the child, the fewer and more basic the shapes must be.
- For very young children, you will need to precut the large shapes. Let the children decorate the shapes with markers for the game.
- Using a ruler may be a new skill for children. You might give them time to practice using it before beginning this activity.

DEVELOPMENTAL GOALS

Develop creativity, small motor development, and hand-eye coordination and explore different uses for markers to tie shape recognition to art.

PREPARATION

Talk about shapes. Begin with the most basic, such as the circle, square, and rectangle. Add more shapes as children learn the basic ones.

PROCESS

1. On construction paper, draw a big shape with markers. Use a ruler to draw straight lines.
2. Cut out the shape.
3. Draw designs and borders on the shape with markers.
4. Place a small piece of double-stick tape on the back of the shape.
5. Stick the shape on the floor.
6. Play "Name That Shape " game.
7. In this game, a leader starts the music. Walk around the room, stepping on different shapes. When the music stops, the leader asks a child to name the shape. That child becomes the next leader.

VARIATIONS

- Use colors, animals, letters, names, or any other concept the children are learning about for this game.
- Add instruments to play during the game.
- Add listening and motor-skill challenges. The children make up directions in advance and write them on cards (e.g., "If you are on a red square, put your hand on your head").

NOTES FOR NEXT TIME: _____

_____

Shape Tracing

MATERIALS

- ☐ common objects (e.g., a fork, a spoon, cup, dish)
- ☐ construction paper
- ☐ markers
- ☐ oak tag or poster board
- ☐ glue
- ☐ clear contact paper (optional)

HELPFUL HINT

- Matching games are good individual activities for children. Sometimes even young children need some alone time.

DEVELOPMENTAL GOALS

Develop creativity, small motor development, and hand-eye coordination and practice grouping and sorting skills.

PREPARATION

Talk about the items collected for this activity. Let the children see and hold the items. Talk about how the items go together. For example, the items are all used at the table when we eat.

PROCESS

1. Place one object on a piece of construction paper and trace around it with a marker.
2. Place another object on the construction paper and trace around it.
3. Continue until all objects have been traced.
4. Use the sheets with the traced objects for a matching game.
5. Have a child select an object from a box and match it to the outline on the paper.
6. Glue the sheet to poster board and cover it with clear contact paper for durability.

VARIATIONS

- Trace around the cardboard shapes or letters. Use them in a matching game.
- Make placemats for lunch or snack time with outlines for cups, napkins, and so on.

NOTES FOR NEXT TIME: _____

_____

Shoebox Crayon Creations

MATERIALS

- ☐ construction paper
- ☐ shoeboxes
- ☐ blunt-tip scissors
- ☐ glue
- ☐ crayons

HELPFUL HINTS

- Expect older children to want to add many details to their shoebox structures. Be sure to have plenty of markers, crayons, and colored pencils available for this purpose.
- Younger children may need help in cutting out the doors and windows on their shoeboxes.

DEVELOPMENTAL GOALS

Develop creativity, small motor development, and hand-eye coordination and encourage recycling.

PREPARATION

Ask parents or friends to collect shoeboxes for this activity. Walk around the neighborhood to observe the kinds of places people live in, where they park their cars, and what kinds of stores can be seen.

PROCESS

1. Cut out construction paper to cover the shoebox.
2. Glue construction paper on the shoebox.
3. Draw windows, a roof, and other features on with crayons.
4. Cut out doors and windows with scissors.

VARIATIONS

- Make a neighborhood of shoebox houses, garages, and stores.
- Add toy cars to drive into the shoebox garages.
- Make shoebox "treasure boxes." Decorate with crayons and markers. Store found objects from walks and other goodies in them.

NOTES FOR NEXT TIME: _____

_____

_____

_____

Sidewalk Chalk

MATERIALS

- ☐ 4 to 5 eggshells
- ☐ 1 teaspoon flour
- ☐ 1 teaspoon very hot tap water
- ☐ food coloring
- ☐ mixing bowl
- ☐ spoon
- ☐ paper towels

HELPFUL HINTS

- This chalk is for sidewalks only. Do not use this chalk on any other surface.
- Be sure to tell the children that the chalk must dry for 3 days before you start the activity. You might circle the day on the calendar when the chalk will be ready to use.
- This recipe makes one large piece of chalk or two smaller pieces.
- Have the children bring in the washed eggshells for this activity.

DEVELOPMENTAL GOALS

Develop creativity, small motor development, and hand-eye coordination and create a new type of chalk.

PREPARATION

Wash and dry the eggshells. Put them in a bowl and grind into a powder. A mortar and pestle works fine for this, or just use the bowl of a large spoon. Discard any large pieces.

PROCESS

1. Place the flour and hot water in another bowl.
2. Add 1 tablespoon eggshell powder and mix until a paste forms.
3. Add food coloring, if desired.
4. Shape and press the mixture firmly into the shape of a chalk stick.
5. Roll up tightly in a strip of paper towel.
6. Allow to dry approximately 3 days until hard.
7. Remove paper towel and you have chalk!

VARIATIONS

- Shape the chalk dough into a round or an oval shape.
- Make chalk with several different colors of food colorings.

NOTES FOR NEXT TIME: _____

_____

_____

Sleep-Time Friends

MATERIALS

- ☐ markers
- ☐ glue
- ☐ blunt-tip scissors
- ☐ grocery bags
- ☐ newspaper
- ☐ yarn (optional)

HELPFUL HINT

- Be sure to emphasize that sleeping is not always necessary at rest time. Just resting is acceptable.

NOTES FOR NEXT TIME:

_____

_____

_____

_____

_____

_____

DEVELOPMENTAL GOALS

Develop creativity, small motor development, and hand-eye coordination and explore a new use of markers.

PREPARATION

Discuss rest time. Ask about things that help the children rest. Talk about favorite blankets or cuddly stuffed animals. Have the children think about what they want to make to help them at rest time. To make grocery bags soft, soak them in water. Crumple the bags and squeeze water through them. Flatten them to dry. This may take a day or two.

PROCESS

1. With markers, draw the shape and size of your sleep-time friend.
2. Make the friend big enough to stuff.
3. Cut two pieces the same size: one for front, and one for back.
4. Decorate both sides with markers.
5. Crumple recycled newspaper for stuffing. Lay the stuffing on the bottom half of the sleep-time friend.
6. Put glue all around the outside edges. Place the top of the sleep-time friend on the stuffing and seal the edges.
7. Dry overnight.
8. Add details with markers or glue yarn around the edges.

VARIATIONS

- Small sleep-time friends can be stuffed with cotton balls or recycled, washed pantyhose.
- Make sleep-time friends out of flannel or muslin. Decorate the friends with fabric crayons. Fill with pillow stuffing.

Splatter Chalk Designs

MATERIALS

☐ colored chalk

☐ plastic pump bottles of different sizes

HELPFUL HINT

• Be prepared for the possibility that some children will enjoy the spraying more than the chalk drawing. Make this a creative experience, too. Challenge the children to come up with different ways to spray water to create different effects on their chalk drawings.

DEVELOPMENTAL GOALS

Develop creativity, small motor development, and hand-eye coordination and explore a new chalk technique.

PREPARATION

Fill the plastic pump bottles with water.

PROCESS

1. Color the sidewalk with colored chalk.
2. Press the pump top and let the water splatter over the chalk on the sidewalk.
3. This makes a splatter design on the chalk.

VARIATIONS

• Use different-sized pump bottles, comparing the different water marks each bottle makes.

• Add food coloring to water in the pump bottles. See what different effects this makes on the chalk drawing.

• Do this activity indoors on sheets of paper with chalk drawings on them. Be sure to prepare the area for lots of water spraying!

NOTES FOR NEXT TIME: _____

_____

_____

_____

Squares

MATERIALS

- ☐ crayons
- ☐ paper

HELPFUL HINT

- This activity is appropriate for children who can identify shapes.

DEVELOPMENTAL GOALS

Develop creativity, small motor development, and hand-eye coordination.

PREPARATION

Talk about squares and how we know things are square because they have four even sides. Discuss how squares are all over the place. Look at these square things.

PROCESS

1. On a piece of paper, draw squares.
2. Draw the squares in different sizes.
3. Try stacking the squares.
4. Draw a design or an object made totally of squares.
5. Color the squares different colors.

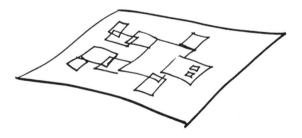

VARIATIONS

- Do the same activity using only circles, triangles, rectangles, ovals, and so on.
- Use markers to add details to the design.
- Glue on scraps of fabric or cloth for added effects.

NOTES FOR NEXT TIME: _____

_____

_____

_____

Stained-Glass Chalk Designs

MATERIALS

- ☐ black construction paper
- ☐ white glue
- ☐ colored chalk
- ☐ examples of stained glass (pictures or the real thing)

HELPFUL HINT

- This is a good activity for children in the basic forms stage of drawing.

DEVELOPMENTAL GOALS

Develop creativity, small motor development, and hand-eye coordination and explore a new chalking technique.

PREPARATION

Show the children pictures of stained glass (or the real thing). Discuss the colors. See how the colors are in separate sections. Talk about the colors and shapes the children see in the stained glass.

PROCESS

1. Create a stained glass design and draw it on the construction paper using white glue.
2. Experiment with different shapes and images.
3. When the glue is dry, color between the glue lines using colored chalks.
4. Adult sprays design with hairspray to prevent the chalk from smudging off the paper.

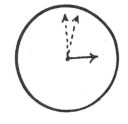

VARIATION

- Try light-colored construction paper and pastel-colored chalks for a very different kind of stained-glass effect.

NOTES FOR NEXT TIME: _____

_____

_____

_____

Starchy Chalk

MATERIALS

- ☐ liquid starch
- ☐ dry chalk
- ☐ paper
- ☐ brush for applying starch
- ☐ water

HELPFUL HINTS

- There is less friction when using chalk on liquid starch. The paper is less likely to tear because of this.
- Liquid starch is available in the grocery store where laundry products are sold.

DEVELOPMENTAL GOALS

Develop creativity, small motor development, and hand-eye coordination and explore new chalk activities.

PREPARATION

Pour the starch into a shallow container. Provide each child with a brush and piece of paper.

PROCESS

1. Brush liquid starch onto the paper.
2. Apply dry chalk to the paper, making a picture or a design.
3. Allow to dry thoroughly.
4. Spray with a fixative to keep from smearing. (Ordinary hairspray works well.) Be sure to spray fixative in a well-ventilated area!

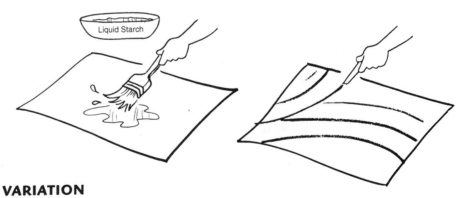

Liquid Starch

VARIATION

- Use different colors of chalk and different kinds of paper.

NOTES FOR NEXT TIME: _____

_____

_____

_____

Sugar and Chalk

MATERIALS

- ☐ sugar
- ☐ water
- ☐ large pieces of chalk
- ☐ paper
- ☐ container for sugar-water mixture

HELPFUL HINT

- Have the sugar-soaked chalk ready when you begin this activity. The children do not enjoy waiting 15 minutes to start this activity.

DEVELOPMENTAL GOALS

Develop creativity, small motor development, and hand-eye coordination and explore new chalk techniques.

PREPARATION

Mix one part sugar and two parts water (e.g., 1/2 cup sugar and 1 cup water).

PROCESS

1. Soak pieces of large chalk in the sugar-water mixture for about 15 minutes.
2. Use the chalk on dry paper.
3. Sugar gives the chalk a shiny look when dry.

VARIATIONS

- Use all light or all dark chalks.
- Use the sugar-soaked chalk on cardboard and recycled white gift boxes.
- Use sugar-soaked white chalk on black construction paper for "snowy" pictures.

NOTES FOR NEXT TIME: _____

_____

_____

_____

3
Years Old and UP

The Adventures of a Line

DEVELOPMENTAL GOALS

Develop creativity, small motor development, and hand-eye coordination and explore the concept of lines using markers.

MATERIALS

☐ flip pad

☐ colored markers

☐ 8-1/2" × 11" sheets of white paper for each child

HELPFUL HINT

• If you lack art books, have the children look for lines in the room or outdoors.

PREPARATION

Review the types of lines with the children. Talk about wavy, straight, zigzag, vertical, horizontal, dotted, and spiral lines. Draw the lines on the flip pad as they are discussed.

PROCESS

1. Using a colored marker, draw a dot on the paper.

2. Have a child make a type of line starting with that dot.

3. Have a child draw many kinds of lines, each starting with a dot.

4. Alternate colors of markers when making lines.

5. Use your favorite line to make a design or picture on another piece of paper.

VARIATIONS

• Create a story using different types of lines (e.g., a line is a dot that went for a walk in the snow). Each set of subsequent lines can be different things (e.g., thin parallel lines are sled tracks, thin curvy lines are a bicycle track, parallel zigzags could be car tires, spiral lines could be a snake track).

• Older children may search art books for types of lines. This can be done as a group in front of a single painting, or the children can be given a card with a type of line and told to search the room for the best example of that type of line.

NOTES FOR NEXT TIME: _____

_____

_____

T-Shirt Crayon Designs

MATERIALS

- ☐ T-shirt (light-colored)
- ☐ wax crayons
- ☐ newspaper
- ☐ iron
- ☐ ironing board (or pieces of heavy cardboard)
- ☐ paper

HELPFUL HINTS

- Be very careful when using an iron around the children. Be sure they stay well away from it during the pressing process.
- The color will last only if the fabric is washed in cool water with a non-detergent soap.

DEVELOPMENTAL GOALS

Develop creativity, small motor development, and hand-eye coordination and explore new uses for crayons.

PREPARATION

Discuss with the children what they would like to draw on their T-shirts. Explain that when they draw on the T-shirt, it will be permanent. They may want to practice their picture or design on paper before drawing it on the T-shirt.

PROCESS

1. Using wax crayons, draw a picture on a white or light-colored T-shirt.

2. The teacher uses an iron to press with newspaper over the picture and on an ironing board or a piece of heavy cardboard.

3. The picture will stay indefinitely.

VARIATIONS

- Fabric crayons are available for drawing on T-shirts. These work very well, but not everyone can afford these in addition to regular crayons!
- If you do have fabric crayons, use them to make designs on white tennis shoes.

NOTES FOR NEXT TIME: _____

_____

_____

_____

Yarn and Marker Fun

MATERIALS

- ☐ recycled yarn
- ☐ markers
- ☐ glue
- ☐ construction paper
- ☐ ruler

HELPFUL HINTS

- This is an appropriate activity for children who are learning their letters.
- For children who are not yet at letter recognition, use shapes instead.

DEVELOPMENTAL GOALS

Develop creativity, small motor development, and hand-eye coordination and explore a new use for markers while making letters.

PREPARATION

Cut the yarn into 24" pieces. (Older children may use a ruler to measure and cut their own yarn.)

PROCESS

1. Choose a piece of yarn.
2. Shape the yarn into a letter. Make another letter.
3. Make a letter with glue on colored construction paper.
4. Glue the yarn to the paper. Dry overnight.
5. Trace around the yarn letter with markers. Trace several times with different colors.
6. Make other interesting designs around the letter.

VARIATIONS

- Use yarn with a flannel board. It sticks well and is fun for open-ended, creative designing.
- Lay the yarn on letters, such as on newspaper headlines or poster titles.
- Have the children work in pairs. One child names a letter and the other shapes it with yarn.

NOTES FOR NEXT TIME: _____

_____

_____

_____

Index by Ages